# Honeycatchers

## Alishea Clark

BookLeaf Publishing

India | USA | UK

Honeycatchers © 2023 Alishea Clark

All rights reserved.

No part of this publication may be reproduced, stored in a retrieval system, or transmitted, in any form or by any means, electronic, mechanical, photocopying, recording or otherwise, without the prior written permission of the presenters.

Alishea Clark asserts the moral right to be identified as author of this work.

Presentation by *BookLeaf Publishing*

Web: www.bookleafpub.com

E-mail: info@bookleafpub.com

ISBN: 9789358735598

First edition 2023

*This collection is dedicated to everyone
who will not read it, because they are afraid
they might see themselves in it.*


*For Michael, my brother & almost-twin. I
miss you so much*


*For everyone who misses being loved*

# ACKNOWLEDGEMENT

First, and most importantly - I want to thank myself, for sticking around. Through everything.

Finally, thank you, for picking up this little collection of thoughts and things. I hope you love it

# PREFACE

I am sorry if you don't like poetry. I am also sorry if you do like poetry, because often times it is sad, and I am sorry that you are hurting too.

If you don't know how to read poetry, try it slowly, try it loudly, try it when it's raining, like it's bitter sips of coffee. Not rushed like morning coffee, no - slow like evening coffee. Try it crying, or laughing. Just try it - it might make you feel something.

# Bluebottle

Pin me like a butterfly
with wings splayed
exposed and vulnerable

Take me in, slowly now
I am a fleeting thing.
Anchor your gaze to mine
Commit me to memory

Cetacean and juniper
A tempest and fiery absinthe
Do you see me now?

Hold me in place,
drown me in your regard
Keep me here, collect me
I am a curio, a rare find

Pull the breath from me,
imprint yourself in it's place
reshape my very being

eyes burning and hearts beating
lose yourself in me
You will not want to be found

# Snowdrop - For Emma

Grow tall little wildflower
Do not let this world keep you small
Wind will come,
rain will fall,
let it
know that your roots are mighty

Grow strong, little wildflower
Bloom without hesitation
nothing can bury you,
You yield the stars in your heart

Grow bravely, little wildflower
Do not become small,
for those who refuse to grow
Do not shrink for their comfort

Remember the light that lives in you
Remember the strength in which you grew
Stand tall little wildflower

# A Dying Thing

There is a darkness within some,
it resides within me
clouding thoughts,
cluttering my consciousness
blackening and blurring my vision

it distorts this reality
clawing at wrists
tightening throats
it is dangerous, this darkness
it is harsh, and it is tempting

It is a darkness that soothes,
it is the promise of an end
to the clouded thoughts
the clawed wrists

it is a darkness that gives way to jealousy,
of the wilting flowers,
of falling leaves,
it is a jealousy of dying things

Time passes,
we continue to deny it
"not today" I tell myself,
I am no dying thing

# Call it Greed

I will accept what i deserve
and i will ask for more
always more
Every last good thing
That this universe can give me
I will selfishly take for myself.
I will not keep low standards,
i will not accept good enough
i will demand more of what my heart screams
for
i will be my own source of pleasure and joy
I will be my own sun and moon

# Do you want to go to bed?

a nod of anticipation
and a grin of expectation
the soft brush of lips on collarbone
fingertips on skin
a road map for lips to follow

touch me,
take me to places i cannot write about
I'm all yours, darling
I'm all yours
I'll pay close attention to every detail in your
breath
every trace of your tongue
the scent of your skin
the weight of your body on mine
your body on mine

worship at the altar of me
I want to feel my name on your breath
repeat it like an incantation

Mark me, make me yours
skin against skin
sweat soaking into sweat
heavy breaths and tangled sheets

show me how to sleep with you
heartbeats racing
lips and bodies moving slowly together
whisper something sweet and take me

make me think of you tomorrow,
and tomorrow,
and tomorrow.

We are spent, though i still want more of you
I am not ready to go to sleep

"Time goes, you say? Ah no,
alas, time stays, we go." -
Henry Austin Dobson

What has died;
My apple watch, my first cat, my childhood and
most of my family. Figuratively of course, as
they are all breathing somewhere. Which is to
say they are alive in someone's life, somewhere
I'm sure.
What has died;
The economy, and therefore my predilection for
original art and handmade soap. My love for
you. The part of me that allowed me to love you.
Me in the future. Me in other timelines
everything that will not, no, can not be. My
brother. My grandmothers. The you in my head.
The me in my head. The you and me that I made
you and me in my head.
Everything that is not in this moment.
Everything in our future.
There is never enough time

# Untitled I

You say you hate the thought
of someone else touching me
loving me
experiencing me
but i often wonder if truly,
you hate the role you played
in someone else's having me
Perhaps you look at me with them
and see all of the small ways you fucked up
each push you gave me
each harsh word, a nudge in another direction .
It is true that i left you,
but it was long after you'd abandoned me
watched me cry, and yell, and beg
watched me open my own veins
I left you, yes,
because you watched me slowly burn out, and
made no effort to reignite my fire
I am my own kindling and flame now
watch me burn without you
you will see,
my heat will warm other hands,
and they will not shy away like cowards
You were cruel with my sadness.
I let you go.

# Untitled II

I ask the universe questions and she sends me
rain, blackberries, pink skies,
 answers i haven't figured out the meaning of
yet.
I ask her how you're doing and she sends me
crows on my streetlight,
deeply colored sunsets, fireflies, and folk music.
She sends me my favorite things.
Tiny joys that memories of you do not bleed into
Reminders of myself
of why I do not need you.
I ask the universe how to forget you,
how to get you out of my goddamn head.
How to return to the me before the you.
How to let go of the me without the you
She sends me quiet hikes,
half-lit joints and songbirds
Downpour while i walk back to my car

So i ask the universe what to do with it.
 Where can I carry an ache for someone who is
not, will not, be there.
She sends me fingers drumming on steering
wheels,

american bar food, and ice cubes in my bong
hits
She sends me rock music, and full moons, and
telescopes.
Each new thing a new ache in my chest.
"You carry these here" she says
"with the fireflies, and the folk music, and the
other sacred things
I will miss you
and the world will move forward

She sends me self-reflection.
There is no me before you now.
There is only me.

How extraordinary

# CPTSD and Poor Memory

I don't always remember things. Something
about a trauma response i'm told.
When I love a person, i keep them in my pocket.
In a note under their name, listing all of their
favorite things.
Rose loves Big Hero 6,  and Frank LLoyd
Wright
Kate loves things with mushrooms on them
My brother loves reese's, and the doritos in the
purple bag.
I deleted the note with your name on it,
on the same day that I blocked you, and deleted
every picture I took of you.
(i take pictures of every happy thing, because I
don't always remember things)
You told me that you liked when i took your
picture. It made you feel seen.
I took so many pictures, hoping you'd see me
too.
I deleted everything under your shadow,
and I still remember your favorite things
Dijon mustard pretzels
late night PC gaming
compliments on hard days.
I erased every digital memory of you

because I want them out of my head
Because I want you out of my head.
I still remember your favorite things

# If you ever think of me (or feel like reaching out)

Spare me your careless hands,
your wandering feet
I have torn you from my atoms
and exorcised you from this heart
Do not dig up what I have buried.
I am trying to burn the very memory of you
from my thoughts
I have done well,
I wish you could see
I am trying so hard to forget you ever existed
be patient with me,
it is hard to remove someone from your soul
when your fingers are still trembling.

# How Delusional

You left your hoodie in my car
I didn't return it after you jumped ship.
I willed it to be an anchor,
to bring you back to me
how delusional

# In Tarot, water represents emotion

I've grown tired of being told that I am too
much
give me a person who can handle my quiet
streams
and my turbulent white rapids
give me someone who won't leave
when they discover how much i bubble over
someone who will let me pour, and will cup their
hands
to hold me,
to feel me run through them
Not someone who is afraid of my current
give me another wild soul,
with hands that do not grasp,
with feet that chase
give me someone who wants too much

# Things I didn't know that I loved, until I loved you

Guacamole - I make the best. (I stole your recipe)
Kissing and whispering things
King Palms and playing chess
East coast accents, and getting lost on hikes

Late night drives to secret places
Heated blankets, and the love I felt
when you always had it warming my side of the bed
Hockey games, and late night talks about intimate things
Those intimate things.

My eyes.
The intensity of the way I love
This body
Everything it has done for me
My mind, and the opportunity you gave me to grow,
To heal

# August feels like bleeding

Like being stuck in a nostalgia so vivid,
So potent.
August is for longing
For homesickness, and sentimentality

For memories of catching fireflies,
of picking (eating) all of Grandma's black
raspberries
memories of long bike rides on golden days
Sun tanned skin, and sun bleached hair
The smell of tea tree oil for our sunburns

August is for playing house.
For listening for locusts,
And always telling mom when we hear them for
the first time.
I still do.

August is a dull ache in my heart
at the sight of starlings migrating
their dark murmurations dancing with the pink
sunsets
now earlier each day
It's cloudy more, and the fireflies have gone.

August feels like the last hum of electricity,
when you unplug an old TV

August feels like missing you more.

-For Michael

# This isn't about mascara

I had a mascara that I loved for many years.
It was my first, and I knew that I didn't want any
other.
I was so in love with it, the brightest part of my
morning,
It became unhealthy, and I had to let it go.
I keep trying to find one like it, but I don't know
that it exists,
I haven't worn mascara in a long time, and it's
hard
My cat still thinks I'm pretty,
With or without mascara

# Whispered things

You whispered
"May I"
and my breath caught in my chest
no one else had ever asked

# Pink

In another universe the sky is always pink,
and I didn't lose myself loving you,
and in another one the clouds grow downwards
to kiss the sea,
and in one we meet in your backyard, we are six
and we are chasing the same firefly

# When I fall for someone

22

I do not simply fall - I collapse
It is messy,
and chaotic,
and nearly always leaves me bleeding
like i am a grain of sand, and the entire beach
like another version of me, that will not make it
like a dawn, and a death.
No when I fall for someone, I do not simply fall
I fall with a love that can consume,
a love that consumes me in return,

# You tied our souls together

23

I really loved that version of myself,
I think I mourn her more than I mourn you.
So I look at the moon, and I'm not happy.
I am not sure it is something I can be.
We are here, with all this chemistry,
but a space between us that cannot be breached.
I will keep your sun in my heart,
I will tell myself that it isn't my fault,
that some people don't have the same intensity
as you.

# Tell me how you love me

Tell me I am a daisy,
and I will bloom for you.
Tell me I am a raincloud,
and find yourself in my storm.
Tell me I am an earthquake,
I will show you how I tremble

Tell me I am yours,
and see me bare my flaws.
Tell me that I am birdsong,
and listen to my melody
Tell me that I am a wildfire,
and stand back while I burn

Tell me how you love me,
and see how I unravel.
Tell me you are mine,
and I will become the very thing
you have always needed

# The Deepest Breath

Being with you felt like being alone,
like holding myself,
collapsing into myself.

Being with you taught me things.
like how to smile while drowning,
how to kick, and to thrash,
how to catch my breath,
while you dragged me under

Being with you taught me things,
like loving myself,
comforting myself,
complimenting myself.

The fight to breathe,
the struggle to survive you,
was a gift from you.
You gave me the strength to force your grip from
me,
To pull your hands from my throat,
my mind, my heart, my body.
To push off the bottom of
the harsh floor of your dark depths
You gifted me the strength

to dive away from you,
to hold myself,
collapse into myself.

I can breathe here,
In this space where you do not drown me

www.ingramcontent.com/pod-product-compliance
Lightning Source LLC
LaVergne TN
LVHW010843200726
843508LV00012B/2725